BEI GRIN MACHT SICH
WISSEN BEZAHLT

Martin Steinert

Wirtschaftsmediation - Eine Alternative im organisationalen Konfliktmanagement?

GRIN Verlag

Bibliografische Information der Deutschen Nationalbibliothek:

Die Deutsche Bibliothek verzeichnet diese Publikation in der Deutschen National-
bibliografie; detaillierte bibliografische Daten sind im Internet über http://dnb.d-
nb.de/ abrufbar.

Dieses Werk sowie alle darin enthaltenen einzelnen Beiträge und Abbildungen
sind urheberrechtlich geschützt. Jede Verwertung, die nicht ausdrücklich vom
Urheberrechtsschutz zugelassen ist, bedarf der vorherigen Zustimmung des Verla-
ges. Das gilt insbesondere für Vervielfältigungen, Bearbeitungen, Übersetzungen,
Mikroverfilmungen, Auswertungen durch Datenbanken und für die Einspeicherung
und Verarbeitung in elektronische Systeme. Alle Rechte, auch die des auszugsweisen
Nachdrucks, der fotomechanischen Wiedergabe (einschließlich Mikrokopie) sowie
der Auswertung durch Datenbanken oder ähnliche Einrichtungen, vorbehalten.

Impressum:

Copyright © 2011 GRIN Verlag GmbH
Druck und Bindung: Books on Demand GmbH, Norderstedt Germany
ISBN: 978-3-656-07027-6

Dieses Buch bei GRIN:

http://www.grin.com/de/e-book/182988/wirtschaftsmediation-eine-alternative-im-
organisationalen-konfliktmanagement

GRIN - Your knowledge has value

Der GRIN Verlag publiziert seit 1998 wissenschaftliche Arbeiten von Studenten, Hochschullehrern und anderen Akademikern als eBook und gedrucktes Buch. Die Verlagswebsite www.grin.com ist die ideale Plattform zur Veröffentlichung von Hausarbeiten, Abschlussarbeiten, wissenschaftlichen Aufsätzen, Dissertationen und Fachbüchern.

Besuchen Sie uns im Internet:

http://www.grin.com/

http://www.facebook.com/grincom

http://www.twitter.com/grin_com

Wirtschaftsmediation –

eine Alternative im organisationalen Konfliktmanagement?

Hausarbeit

vorgelegt von

Name: Martin Steinert

Studiengang: BA Bildungs- und Erziehungswissenschaft

Trimester: 6. Trimester / FT 2011

Seminar: Erwachsenenbildung und Organisation - Mediation

Inhalt

1   Einleitung 2

2   Begriffsdefinitionen 3

    2.1   sozialer Konflikt 3

    2.2   Konfliktmanagement 4

    2.3   Mediation 5

3   Wirtschaftsmediation – eine Alternative 6

    3.1   Abgrenzung zu anderen Konfliktmanagementverfahren 6

    3.2   Inhalte der Wirtschaftsmediation 7

       3.2.1   Besonderheiten der Arbeitswelt 8

       3.2.1   Besonderheiten von Organisationen 8

    3.3   Ablauf einer Wirtschaftsmediation 9

    3.4   Stärken und Schwächen der Wirtschaftsmediation 11

4   Zusammenfassung 12

5   Schluss 13

6   Literaturverzeichnis 14

1 Einleitung

„Streitende sollten wissen, daß nie einer ganz recht hat und der andere ganz unrecht." (*Kurt Tocholsky*, o.J.)

Dieses Zitat des Schriftstellers Kurt Tocholsky beschreibt treffend die häufig auftretende Problematik eines Konfliktes innerhalb, beziehungsweise zwischen sozialen Gruppen oder einzelnen Personen. Überall dort, wo Menschen mit verschiedenen Wertevorstellungen, Interessen und persönlichen Zielen zusammentreffen sind Konflikte auf lange Sicht nicht vermeidbar. Innerhalb von Organisationen jedoch, welche wirtschaftliche Prinzipien verfolgen, bedeutet ein solcher Konflikt nicht selten eine Unterbrechung des „täglichen ziel- und aufgabenbezogenen Handelns" (*Eilles-Matthiessen* 2005, S. 175) und damit die Gefahr des Misslingens geplanter Ziele und den Verlust aller eingesetzten Ressourcen. Durch ein gezieltes Konfliktmanagement versucht die Organisation einen Einfluss auf den Verlauf bestehender Konflikte zu nehmen.

In der vorliegenden Arbeit soll hierfür die Wirtschaftsmediation, eine relativ neue Methode des Konfliktmanagements, vorgestellt und unter folgender Fragestellung bertrachtet werden: Stellt das Mediationsverfahren im wirtschaftlichen Kontext eine geeignete Alternative zu bestehenden Instrumenten des Konfliktmanagements dar?

Im folgenden Gliederungspunkt werden die im Zusammenhang dieser Arbeit notwendigen Begriffe erläutert. Dafür werde ich klären, was ein sozialer Konflikt ist und welche Formen er annehmen kann, was unter Konfliktmananagement innerhalb von Organisationen zu verstehen ist und was mit einem Mediationsverfahren, speziell der Wirtschaftsmediation gemeint ist.

Im dritten Gliederungspunkt, dem Hauptteil dieser Arbeit, beginne ich mit einer Abgrenzung der Mediation zu anderen Instrumenten des Konfliktmanagements. Unter Betrachtung der kontextualen Besonderheiten von Wirtschaftsmediation werde ich in den folgenden zwei Unterpunkten die Inhalte eines solchen Verfahrens und den Ablauf einer Mediation beleuchten. Den Hauptteil schließt eine Darstellung von Stärken und Schwächen eines Wirtschaftsmediationsverfahrens ab.

Nach einer kurzen Zusammenfassung der gesamten Ausarbeitung soll im Schlussteil die leitende Fragestellung einer kritischen Würdigung und einem persönlichen Resümee unterzogen werden.

2 Begriffsdefinitionen

Aufgrund des Umfanges der vorliegenden Arbeit können die folgenden Begrifflichkeiten nicht aus unterschiedlichen Perspektiven erläutert werden, sondern erfahren ausschließlich eine für das Verständnis relevante definitorische Einordnung.

2.1 sozialer Konflikt

Nicht jede auftretende Differenz ist gleich ein Konflikt und nicht jede Differenz muss sich zu einem Konflikt entwickeln. Schaffen es die Beteiligten ihre sachlichen oder persönlichen Differenzen auf eine akzeptable Lösung zu bringen, wurde ein Konflikt vermieden. Eine Differenz entwickelt sich erst dann zu einem Konflikt, wenn mindestens zwei Personen an der Differenz beteiligt sind und mindestens eine Person eine Beeinträchtigung aus dieser erfährt.

Friedrich Glasl definiert einen sozialen Konflikt als „eine Interaktion zwischen Aktoren (Individuen, Gruppen, Organisationen, Völker usw.). Dabei erlebt wenigstens ein Aktor Differenzen (Unterschiede, Widersprüche oder Unvereinbarkeiten) im Wahrnehmen und im Denken, Vorstellen, Interpretieren, im Fühlen (Sympathie, Antipathie, Vertrauen oder Misstrauen etc.) und im Wollen (Motive, Ziele, Triebfedern) mit dem anderen Aktor (bzw. den anderen Aktoren) und zwar in der Art, dass beim Verwirklichen (Umsetzen, Ausführen, Realisieren) dessen, was der Aktor denkt fühlt oder will eine Beeinträchtigung – durch einen anderen Aktor (bzw. durch die anderen Aktoren) erfolge." (*Glasl* 2003, S. 123)

Überträgt man diese Konfliktvorstellung in eine wirtschaftliche Perspektive stellen sich die Differenzen zwischen den Konfliktparteien oftmals durch die unterschiedlichen Eigeninteressen dar. Die Konfliktparteien verfolgen ausschließlich jene Ziele, welche zu persönlichen Nutzen- und Gewinnmaximierung dienen. Unter der Annahme, der Mensch handle wirtschaftlich vor allem als Homo Oeconomicus, also als rationaler Egoist, enstehen Konflikte meist dadurch, da der Glaube an den finanziellen Vorteil, das Erreichen eines höheren Ansehens und die Stabilisierung der beruflichen und persönlichen Macht nur mit dem bedingungslosen Durchsetzen des eigenen Willens möglich ist. (Vgl. *Kals/Ittner* 2008, S. 4 f.)

Nach einer deutschen Studie zu betrieblichen Konflikten verbringen Mitarbeiter circa zwölf Prozent ihrer Arbeitszeit mit dem Austragen von Konflikten. (Vgl. *Duve/Eidenmüller/Hacke* 2003, S. 11 f.) Die Kosten sozialer Konflikte innerhalb wirtschaftlicher Organisationen stellen daher einen nicht zu verachtenden Anteil dar. Ziel des Managements kann also nur eine gezielte Einflussnahme auf das Konfliktpotential der Organisationsmitglieder sein.

2.2 Konfliktmanagement

Diese gezielte Einflussnahme ist Aufgabe des Konfliktmanagements. Bezeichnen einige Theorien das Konfliktmanagement eher als präventive Maßnahmen zur Sicherung des übergeordneten Organisationsziels, definiert Glasl Konfliktmanagement als eine Kuration eines bereits bestehenden Konfliktprozesses. „Grundlage des Konfliktmanagements ist, dass Gegensätze wesentliche Elemente des sozialen Lebens sind und die Konfliktparteien erkennen sollen, dass ein destruktiver Umgang mit ihnen nicht förderlich ist und daher Konflikte in eine konstruktive Bahn gelenkt werden sollen." (*Kurray* 2008, S. 10)

Glasl unterscheidet in seinem Ansatz zur Konfliktbearbeitung zwei Grundkriterien der Interventionsmaßnahmen. Zum einen sind es bestimmte Ansatzmomente, welche bei einer Intervention stets zu beachten sind, zum anderen die Differenzierung der Situationsgegebenheiten, an denen sich Interventionsstrategien ausrichten sollten. (Vgl. *Fathi* 2008, S. 13) Der Einsatz einer geeigneten Interventionsmaßnahme wird durch den jeweiligen Grad eines Konflikts bestimmt. Glasl zeigt dafür neun verschiedene Konfliktstufen, welche sich weiter in drei Bereiche unterteilen lassen.

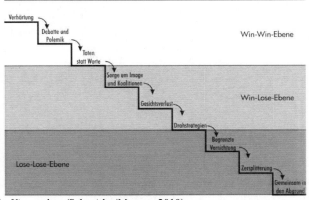

(Abb. *Vigenschow/Schneider/Meyrose* 2010)

Die Konfliktstufen stellen die eigene Wahrnehmungsebene der Streitparteien dar. Dabei ist es durchaus möglich, dass sich die Parteien auf verschiedenen Konfliktstufen befinden.

Das Stufenmodell nach Glasl gibt jedoch keine direkten Interventionshandlungen vor, sondern stellt Handlungsmöglichkeiten der jeweiligen Eskalationsebene dar. (Vgl. *Glasl* 2004, S. 397) In der ersten Eskalationsphase (Stufe eins bis drei) besteht nach Glasl noch ein Kooperationswille zwischen den Streitparteien. Mit gezielter Intervention ist eine beidseitige

Gewinnlösung, eine Win-Win-Strategie, zu erreichen. Dies ist möglich, übernimmt eine Seite der Konfliktparteien die Aufgabe der Streitmoderation und verfolgt Ansätze der Supervision oder der protokolarischen Mediation (Scrivener-Mediation). (Vgl. *Glasl* 2004, S. 404 ff.) Nach Glasl ist es den Konfliktparteien in der zweiten Eskalationsphase (Stufe vier bis sechs) nicht mehr möglich den Streit selbstständig zu klären, da sich der Konflikt von der Sach- auf die Beziehungsebene weiterentwickelte. Die Streitenden verfolgen in dieser Phase eine Win-Lose-Strategie, wobei der Siegende nur so viel gewinnen kann, wie der andere verliert. Glasl schlägt in dieser Konfliktphase die Prozessbegleitung durch Mediation als geeignetes Interventionsinstrument vor. (Vgl. *Ebenda*, S. 409 ff.) In der letzten Eskalationsphase (Stufe sieben bis neun) ist nach Glasl nur noch eine Lose-Lose-Situation zu erreichen. Keine der beiden Konfliktparteien wird einen Vorteil aus dem Streit ziehen können. Geeignete Interventionsmaßnahmen werden hierbei oft durch übergeordnete Machtinstanzen auferlegt und dienen zumeist der Schadensbegrenzung. (Vgl. *Ebenda* 2004, S. 430 ff.)

Zusammenfassend ist daher aufzuzeigen, dass Konfliktmanagement ein strategisches, wohlüberlegtes, zielbezogenes, geplantes und erfolgsorientiertes Herangehen an Konfliktsituationen beschreibt und immer auch die Einstellungen, das Verhalten und die Handlungsoptionen beider Konfliktparteien beachtet. (Vgl. *Selter* 2002, S. 11)

Als eine Interventionsmöglichkeit der zweiten Eskalationsphase schlägt Glasl die Prozessbegleitung mittels Mediation vor. Diese Methode stellt den Schwerpunkt meiner Ausarbeitung dar und soll im folgenden näher erläutert werden.

2.3 Mediation

Die Mediation stellt eine Interventions- und Beratungsform dar, welche erreichen soll, dass „festgefahrene Konflikte und scheinbar unvereinbare Gegensätze zu einer konstruktiven Lösung führen." (*Eilles-Matthiessen* 2005, S. 175)

Der Begriff Mediation bedeutet im angelsächsischen Sprachraum die Vermittlung innerhalb einer Auseinandersetzung (vgl. *Altmann/Müller* 2003, S. 136) und ist als Interventions- und Beratungsverfahren Bestandteil der alternativen Könfliktlösungsmethode (ADR – Alternative Dispute Resolution). Diese alternativen Könfliktlösungsmethoden werden definiert als: „an approach to the settlement of disputes by means other than binding decisions made by courts or tribunals." (*Hamilton* 2010, S.1) Da Konfliktparteien ab einer gewissen Eskalationsstufe nur sehr selten in der Lage sind Probleme und Differenzen direkt zu klären, unterstützt innerhalb der Mediation ein neutrale dritte Person den Konfliktprozess, der Mediator. Ausgangspunkt der Mediation ist die Erkenntnis, „dass Konfliktpartner fähig sind, die für sie akzeptable Lösung gemeinsam zu finden." (*Rebmann* o.J.)

Auf Grundlage der genannten Punkte kann Mediation definiert werden, als ein „außergerichtliches Verfahren zur Lösung eines aktuellen Konflikts, in dem die Konfliktparteien, unterstützt durch einen Mediator, eigenverantwortlich eine tragfähige Konfliktlösung erarbeiten." (*Eilles-Matthiessen* 2005; S. 175) Eine tragfähige Lösung bedeutet hierbei die Herstellung einer zukunftorientierten Win-Win-Situation der Beteiligten. (Vgl. *Adamski* 2009, S. 7)

Die Wirtschaftsmediation übernimmt diese Definition, wobei sich die Konflikte innerhalb dieses Ansatzes speziell im Kontext von Wirtschafts- und Verwaltungsorganisation befinden. (Vgl. *Kals/Ittner* 2008, S. 8)

3 Wirtschaftsmediation – eine Alternative

Zur Lösung bestehender Konflikte kann im Wirtschaftsleben auf eine Vielzahl festgeschriebener Gesetzmäßigkeiten zurückgegriffen werden. Bereiche des Arbeitsrechts, des Gesellschaftsrechts oder spezielle Wirtschaftsrechte (z.B. Patentrecht, Wettbewerbsrecht) können auftretende Konflikte durch ein übergeordnetes Reglement klären. Jedoch sind nicht alle Konflikte innerhalb wirtschaftlicher Organisationen durch solche Gesetzmäßigkeiten geregelt. Besonders ein Konflikt auf Beziehungsebene ist durch die unpersönliche Betrachtung in Folge eines rechtlich ausgetragenen Lösungsansatzes oftmals nur sehr unbefriedigend. Vor allem hier setzten alternative Methoden des Konfliktmanagements an.

3.1 Abgrenzung zu anderen Konfliktmanagementverfahren

Mediation kann mit Blick auf das Vorgehen sowohl gegenüber anderen Beratungsverfahren, wie zum Beispiel Supervision, Moderation oder Coaching, als auch gegenüber anderen Formen des Konfliktlösungsverfahrens abgegrenzt werden. (Vgl. *Eilles-Matthiessen* 2005, S. 177) Im Folgenden werde ich mich auf eine Gegenüberstellung der verschiedenen Verfahren zur Konfliktregelung beschränken. Exemplarisch stelle ich dafür eine Abgrenzung der Mediation zwischen einem Gerichtsverfahren und einer Verhandlung dar. Als Vergleichsdimensionen dienen der Grad der Freiwilligkeit, die Wahl des Vermittlers, der Grad der Formalität des Verfahrens und der Einfluss auf das Prozessergebnis.

Sowohl die Verhandlung als auch die Mediation sind Verfahren, welche die Freiwilligkeit der Streitparteien als Erfolgsvoraussetzung stellen. Nur im Einverständnis aller Beteiligten kann der Konfliktlösungsprozess durchgeführt werden. Während die Verhandlung durch die Konfliktparteien selbst organisiert und durchgeführt wird, benötigt die Mediation einen neutralen Prozessvermittler, den Mediator. Dieser muss von beiden Parteien ausgewählt und akzeptiert werden. Der Mediator dient als Vermittlungsexperte, strukturiert und leitet das Mediationsverfahren ohne dabei jedoch Partei zu ergreifen oder den Prozess selbst zu bestimmen. Das Verhandlungsverfahren dagegen besitzt keine formale Struktur und kann keine Unterstützung durch eine dritte, neutrale Partei nutzen. In der Ergebnisorientierung versuchen beide Konfliktregelungsverfahren, Mediation und Verhandlung, eine für die beteiligten Streitparteien akzeptable Lösung zu finden. (Vgl. *Altmann/Müller* 2003; *Kals/Ittner* 2008)

Das Gerichtsverfahren beruht im Gegensatz zur Mediation auf der Unfreiwilligkeit mindestens einer Streitpartei. Zudem ist es den Beteiligten nicht möglich die Wahl des Vermittlers mitzubestimmen, ausgenommen des eigenen Rechtsbeistandes. Die Prozessordnung reglementiert strikt den Ablauf einer Gerichtsverhandlung, sodass auf die unterschiedlichen Wünsche der Betroffenen nicht eingegangen werden kann. In diesem streng formalisierten Prozess werden die Entscheidungen ausschließlich dahingehend getroffen, welche durch das festgeschriebene Recht vorgegeben sind. Im Gegensatz zur Mediation, in welcher eine Win-Win-Lösung angestrebt wird, endet ein Gerichtsverfahren fast ausschließlich in einer Gewinner-Verlierer-Konstellation. (Vgl. *Altmann/Müller* 2003; *Eilles-Matthiessen* 2005)

3.2 Inhalte der Wirtschaftsmediation

„Die Arbeitswelt ist ein besonderes und auch ein besonders schwieriges Konfliktfeld." (*Kals/Ittner* 2008, S. 45) Die exakten Inhalte einer Wirtschaftmediation darzustellen ist daher nicht möglich, auch vor dem Hintergrund, dass sich grundsätzlich jede Thematik zu einem Konflikt entwickeln kann. Das Einsatzspektrum der Mediation soll anhand der folgenden Aufzählung von Konfliktsituationen verdeutlicht werden:

- Konflikte mit Kunden, Lieferanten und Verbrauchern
- Konflikte zwischen Mitarbeitern, Teams, Abteilungen und anderen Organisationen
- Konflikte zwischen Führungskräften
- Konflikte zwischen Führungskräften und Mitarbeitern
- Konflikte bei Fragen der Haftung und Gewährleistung
- Konflikte bei Fragen der Unternehmensnachfolge
- Konflikte zwischen Unternehmen und Öffentlichkeit

(Vgl. *Haeske* 2003, S. 15)

Konflikte innerhalb von Organisationen des öffentlichen oder wirtschaftlichen Sektors sind häufig gekennzeichnet durch eine hohe Komplexität und einer Vielzahl von Beteiligten. (Vgl. *Haeske* 2003, S. 58; *Eilles-Matthiessen* 2005, S. 184) Aus diesem Grund gilt es einige Besonderheiten der Arbeitswelt und der Organisationen zu beachten.

3.2.1 Besonderheiten der Arbeitswelt

Berufliche Arbeit stellt in der heutigen Gesellschaft die Grundlage zur Erfüllung menschlicher Bedürfnisse dar. Mit ihr können sowohl physiologische Grundbedürfnisse, das Bedürfnis nach Sicherheit, soziale Bedürfnisse, das Bedürfnis nach Anerkennung und auch das Bedürfnis nach Selbstverwirklichung erreicht werden. „Letztlich können alle Bedürfnisse der Bedürfnispyramide nach Maslow durch Arbeit erfüllt werden." (*Kals/Ittner* 2008, S. 45) Berufliche Arbeit ist daher oftmals sehr eng mit der persönlichen Identität des Menschen verbunden. Zudem will man dieses Mittel der Bedürfniserfüllung nicht leichtfertig riskieren. Konflikte jedoch bedeuten auch immer die Angst des beruflichen Scheiterns. „Treten nun Konflikte auf, kommt sehr schnell Angst auf – z.B. Angst um die Sicherung der Existenz und einer Grundsicherung, Angst, sich im persönlich relevanten sozialen Umfeld der Arbeit unbeliebt oder lächerlich zu machen, Angst, dass einem die Wertschätzung entzogen wird oder Angst, zu versagen." (*Ebenda*, S. 46) Durch diesen enormen Einfluss wird klar, welche Auswirkung es haben könnte, bricht eine solch einflussreiche Bedürfnisquelle weg.

Eine weitere Besonderheit der Arbeitswelt wird durch die Komplexität der verschiedenen Bedürfnislagen gekennzeichnet. Es sind eben nicht nur finanzielle Anreize oder die Androhung von Sanktionen, welche das menschliche Verhalten langfristig in eine gewünsche Richtung lenken sondern sehr komplexe Zielvorstellungen die möglichst gut erreicht werden sollten. „Entscheidend ist also der konkrete Umgang mit Konflikten im jeweiligen organisationalen Kontext." (*Ebenda*, S. 46) Der Mediator muss solche Rahmenbedingungen in sein Handen einbeziehen und während des gesamten Prozesses beachten. „Bei der Mediation im Arbeitsleben ist zu beachten, dass die Konfliktparteien in der Regel nach der Bewältigung des aktuellen Konfliktes weiter zusammenarbeiten müssen." (*Eilles-Matthiessen* 2005, S. 184)

3.2.1 Besonderheiten von Organisationen

Auch der Organisationskontext ist durch eine starke Komplexität geprägt. Im Sinne eines systemischen Denkens bedeutet dies, auftretende Konflikte differenziert zu betrachten und die verschiedenen Ebenen innerhalb einer Organisation in die Problemanalyse mit einzubeziehen.

Systemtheoretiker schreiben einer Organisation als soziales System folgende Analysemerkmale zu:

- Personen des sozialen Systems,
- subjektive Deutungen
- soziale Regeln
- Regelkreise
- die materielle und soziale Umwelt,
- die Entwicklung des sozialen Systems.

(Vgl. *König/Volmer* 2008, S. 46 ff.)

Auch im Mediationsverfahren gilt es anfangs herauszustellen, wer die Personen im sozialen System sind, welche Rollen sie innerhalb des Systems einnehmen und inwieweit sie am Konflikt beteiligt sind. Die Analyse der subjektiven Deutungen stellt einen weiteren wichtigen Schritt dar. Im Mediationsverfahren ist das Aufdecken der individuellen Sichtweisen aller Beteiligten die Grundlage der Konfliktbearbeitung. „Dabei ist gerade im Konfliktgeschehen zu beachten, dass keine Subjektive Deutung wahrer oder richtiger ist als die andere." (*Kals/Ittner* 2008, S. 47) Um ein Konfliktfall positiv zu verändern muss zudem eine Analyse der sozialen Regeln erfolgen. Die Schwierigkeit besteht darin, die impliziten und dysfunktionalen Regeln des Systems aufzudecken und zu verändern. Auch fest strukturierte Regelkreise behindern zumeist einen Konfliktlösungsprozess, denn die Unterbrechung eingespielter Verhaltensweisen stellt immer nur eine Ausnahme des Systems dar. Als weitere Analysemerkmale sind die materielle und soziale Systemumwelt sowie die Systementwicklung zu nennen. Technische und soziale Einflüsse auf das System von außen, nehmen Einfluss auf die Entwicklung des Systems und damit auch auf die Entwicklung des Konfliktverlaufes. (Vgl. *Ebenda*, S. 47 f.)

Dieser Überblick verdeutlicht die Wichtigkeit einer umfassenden Systemanalyse und ihre Bedeutung für den Konflikt. Es ist die Aufgabe des Mediators innerhalb der Wirtschaftsmediation „den Blick sowohl auf das Gesamtsystem als auch auf die einzelnen Teilsysteme und Hierarchieebenen zu richten." (*Eilles-Matthiessen* 2005, S. 184)

3.3 Ablauf einer Wirtschaftsmediation

Im folgenden Gliederungspunkt soll ein kurzer Überblick über den Ablauf eines Mediationsverfahrens im wirtschaftlichen Kontext gegeben werden. In der Mediationsliteratur sind eine Vielzahl von Phasenmodellen erläutert, welche den Konfliktbearbeitungsprozess in drei oder sogar mehr als zehn Phasen einteilen. (Vgl. *Troja & Meuer* 2005, S. 226) „Für den Ablauf einer Mediation gibt es keine rechtlichen Regeln oder formalen Einschränkungen." (*Eilles-Matthiessen* 2005, S. 188) Im Folgenden werde ich mich daher auf das Phasenmodell nach Montada und Kals berufen. Diese teilen das Mediationsverfahren in sechs aufeinander folgende Abschnitte ein:

1. Vorbereitung
2. Probleme erfassen und Analysieren
3. Konfliktanalyse
4. Konflikte und Probleme bearbeiten
5. Mediationsvereinbarung
6. Evaluation und Follow-up

(Vgl. *Ebenda*, S. 188)

Die Vorbereitungsphase dient als Orientierungsphase für den Mediator. Seine Aufgabe ist es hierbei, das Konfliktfeld kennenzulernen, die Parteien des Mediationsverfahrens zusammenzustellen und die Ziele dieser Methode zu klären, die rechtlichen Grundlagen und Verfahrensregeln zu erläutern und die Rahmenbedingungen (Zeit, Kosten etc.) zu verhandeln. Die Vorbereitungsphase schließt mit einem von allen Beteiligten akzeptierten Mediationsvertrag ab. (Vgl. *Ebenda*, S. 184)

Die zweite Phase ist gekennzeichnet durch die Analyse der bestehenden Probleme und die Erarbeitung der erwünschten Ziele, die mit einem Konflikt beabsichtigt werden. Es gilt zu eruieren, „welche Bedingungen den Konflikt entstehen, eskalieren und anhalten lassen" (*Ebenda*, S. 191) und welche Ziele oder mögliche Gewinne hinter der Konfliktsituation stecken.

In der Phase der Konfliktanalyse wird versucht die Tiefenstruktur des Konfliktes zu durchdringen. „Es soll herausgearbeitet werden, welche Anliegen der Parteien im Konflikt stehen, wie die Verantwortlichkeit eingeschätzt wird und warum der Konflikt noch nicht beigelegt werden konnte." (*Ebenda*, S. 191)

Die vierte Phase beschreibt die Generierung möglicher Lösungsansätze. Der Mediator übernimmt in dieser Phase die Interessensvermittlung beider Parteien und muss auf mögliche Gemeinsamkeiten in den Lösungsvorschlägen achten. Sich annähernde Lösungsansätze bilden das Fundament von Lösungen, welche von beiden Seiten akzeptiert werden können. (Vgl. *Ebenda*, S. 192)

Mit der Mediationsvereinbarung beginnt die Abschlussphase des Konfliktprozesses. Aus den erarbeiteten Lösungsansätzen soll nun die bestmögliche Handlungsoption ausgewählt und umgesetzt werden. In der Wirtschaftmediation wird diese Vereinbarung oftmals in Form eines rechtsfähigen Vertrages aufgestellt. Innerhalb dieser schriftlich festgehaltenen Vereinbarung ist zusätzlich auch die Umsetzung, beziehungsweise die Implementierung der vereinbarten Neuerungen und deren Kontrollmöglichkeit geregelt. (Vgl. *Eilles-Matthiessen* 2005, S. 193)

Die Evaluationsphase am Ende des Mediationsverfahrens stellt eine Kontrollmöglichkeit dar, ob die Vereinbarungen der Beteiligten vertragsgerecht eingehalten werden. Zudem besteht in dieser Phase auch die Möglichkeit der Evaluation des vollzogenen Mediationsprozesses und der Aufstellung einer Kosten-Ertrags-Bilanz. Die notwendige Datensammlung sollte in einzelnen Evaluationsprozessen während des gesamten Verfahrens stattfinden. (Vgl. *Ebenda*, S. 193 f.)

3.4 Stärken und Schwächen der Wirtschaftsmediation

Zum Abschluss der Betrachtung des Wirtschaftsmediationskonzeptes sollen nachstehend noch die wichtigsten Vor- und Nachteile dieses Ansatzes aufgezeigt werden.

Die im Wirtschaftsleben interessanten Fragen zur Mediation sind oftmals: Wie hoch sind die Kosten einer Mediation und lohnt sich ein solches Verfahren im Gegensatz zu herkömmlichen Konfliktlösungsmethoden? Die Literatur schreibt der Mediation einen hohen ökonomischen Vorteil zu, wobei gesagt werden muss, dass die Kosten eines Mediationsverfahrens eine sehr schwierig zu berechnende Größe darstellen. Obwohl auch die Mediation ein enorme Zeitspanne einnehmen kann, belegen empirische Daten eine Zeitersparnis gegenüber gerichtlich verhandelter Konflikte. „Während das Gerichtsverfahren oftmals lange Wartezeiten auf den Prozessbeginn, eine Streitausfechtung über mehrere Instanzen und gegebenenfalls sogar die Führung mehrerer verschiedener Gerichtsprozesse aufgrund eines einzigen Konflikts befürchten lässt, kann ein Mediationsverfahren beginnen, sobald sich die Parteien über die Durchführung einer Mediation sowie auf eine bestimmte Person als Mediator geeinigt haben." (*Weitz* 2008, S. 77)

Zudem ist die Mediation als ein hoch wirksames Verfahren einzustufen. Die Erfolgsquoten einer Mediation im Wirtschaftbereich liegen geschätzt zwischen 60 und 90 Prozent. (Vgl. *Kals/Ittner* 2008, S. 17) Damit erreicht die Mediation aus ökonomischer Perspektive einen hohe Grad an Effektivität und Effizienz.

Neben den Vorteilen im Kostensektor erreicht die Mediation auch Zugewinne im menschlichen und zwischenmenschlichen Bereich. Das Mediationsverfahren arbeitet gezielt mit den Soft-Skills der Beteiligten, also mit deren sozialer Kompetenz. Die Konfliktparteien erarbeiten ihre Lösungsansätze selbst und sind maßgeblich für den Erfolg und den positiven Ausgang der Mediation verantwortlich. Dafür müssen sie sowohl Zugeständnisse gegenüber der anderen Partei machen als auch den eigenen Willen zum durchsetzen sehr relevanter Punkte bekunden. Bei einer erfolgreichen Mediation kann von einer Ergebniszufriedenheit beider Konfliktparteien ausgegangen werden. „Diese wahrgenommene Effizienz und Zufriedenheit stärken das Vertrauen und die Beziehung zu anderen Konfliktpartei und in das Unternehmen als Ganzes." (*Kals/Ittner* 2008, S. 19)

Neben den Vorteilen des verbesserten Verhältnisses zwischen den Konfliktparteien bringt das Mediationsverfahren auch persönliche Vorteile für die Beteiligten. Die selbsterarbeitete Lösungsstrategie entwickelt eine neue Art der Konfliktlösungskompetenz. „The very process of [...] mediation can be an educational one that may help the parties to learn how to handle conflicts better and hence to be able to resolve future disputes more effectively by themselves." (*Weitz* 2008, S. 92 zit. n. *Sander* 2000)

Natürlich bürgt ein solches Verfahren auch Prozessschwächen. Ein Nachteil des Mediationsverfahrens betrifft die zu entrichtenden Kosten. Zwar liegen die Gesamtkosten einer erfolgreichen Mediation meist unter denen eines Gerichtsverfahrens, doch ändert sich dies wenn eine Mediation ohne Erfolg endet und abgebrochen werden muss. Ein weiterer Nachteil stellt die Möglichkeit dar das Mediationsverfahren und die darin vermittelten Informationen als Vorbereitung auf eine juristische Austragung des Konfliktes zu nutzen. (Vgl. *Ebenda*, S. 93)

Zusammenfassend lässt sich zeigen, dass die Mediationsvorteile dessen Nachteile deutlich überwiegen und zum verbreiteten Interesse gegenüber dieser Konfliktmanagementmethode beitragen.

4 Zusammenfassung

Konflikte sind fester Bestandteil unseres privaten und beruflichen Alltags. Vor allem innerhalb wirtschaftlich agierender Organisationen bedeutet ein erfolgreiches Aufarbeiten solcher Konflikte verbesserte Chancen langfristig am Markt zu bestehen. Ein professionelles Konfliktmanagement ist für viele Betriebe daher unverzichtbar. Die Mediation stellt dafür eine Möglichkeit dar, Konflikte auch außergerichtlich und für beide Streitparteien ohne Verlust zu lösen. „Der Mediator führt die Konfliktparteien durch einen Klärungsprozess, der sie befähigt, ihre eigenen Interessen und diejenigen der andren Partei zu verstehen, um gemeinsam eine einvernehmliche Lösung zu finden." (*Eilles-Matthiessen* 2005, S. 176) Im wirtschaftlichen Kontext sind dafür einige Besonderheiten des Arbeitslebens und der Organisation zu beachten.

5 Schluss

Anhand der thematischen Bearbeitung lässt sich feststellen, dass die einleitend gestellt Frage, ob das Mediationsverfahren eine geeignete Alternative zu bestehenden Konfliktmanagementinstrumenten darstellt, mit ja zu beantworten ist.

Im wirtschaftlichen Kotext sticht eine Methode, welche Konflikte ohne einseitige Verlierer lösen kann als denkbar Beste heraus. Solange Differenzen auf eine solche Art und Weise geklärt werden können und dabei noch Vorteile für die gesamte Organisation und den einzelnen Beteiligten entstehen, erachte ich die Mediation als das wertvollste Mittel eines strategischen Konfliktmanagements.

Dennoch sei zu bedenken, dass die Mediation kein Allheilmittel darstellt und „dass sich nicht jeder Fall zur Durchführung einer Mediation eignet, so dass die Mediation schon aufgrund des Vorbehalts der Falleignung nur eine sinnvolle Ergänzung, nicht aber einen [vollständigen] Ersatz für die herkömmlichen Methoden zur Konfliktbeilegung (…) darstellen kann." (*Weitz* 2008, S. 75)

Im Zuge des Seminars konnte ich ein großes Interesse für diesen Bereich der Organisationsberatung entwickeln. Die vertiefende Auseinandersetzung innerhalb dieser Ausarbeitung bestätigte dieses Interesse. Ich sehe die Mediation als ein sehr fortschrittliches Instrument Konflikte vorteilhaft und zukunftsorientiert zu lösen. Die zunehmende berufliche Orientierung und Spezialisierung von Juristen, Personalern und Beratern im Bereich Mediation bestätigt mich in dieser Annahme.

6 Literaturverzeichnis

Adamski, C. (2009). *Wirtschaftsmediation im Vergleich zum Zivilprozess: Eine Gegenüberstellung beider Konfliktlösungsverfahren.* Hamburg: Diplomica-Verlag.

Altmann, G., & Müller, R. (2003). Mediation. In E. Auhagen, & H.-W. Bierhoff, *Angewandte Sozialpsychologie: Das Praxishandbuch* (S. 136-154). Weinheim, Basel, Berlin: Beltz Verlag.

Duve, C., Eidenmülle, H., & Hacke, A. (2003). *Mediation in der Wirtschaft.* Köln: C.H. Beck Verlag.

Eilles-Matthiessen, C. (2005). Mediation: Konflikte konstruktiv bewältigen. In C. Eilles Mathiessen, & S. Janssen, *Beratungskompass: Grundlagen von Coaching, Karriereberatung, Outplacement und Mediation* (S. 175-202). Offenbach: Gabal-Verlag.

Fathi, K. P. (2008). *Möglichkeiten der Integration unterschiedlicher Methoden mediativer Konfliktbearbeitung: Ein konzeptioneller Vorschlag.* Hamburg: Diplomica Verlag.

Glasl, F. (2003). Konfliktmanagement. In A. E. Auhagen, & H.-W. Bierhoff, *Angewandte Sozialpsychologie: Das Praxishandbuch* (S. 123-134). Weinheim, Basel, Berlin: Beltz Verlag.

Glasl, F. (2004). *Konfliktmanagement: Ein Handbuch für Führungskräfte, Beraterinnen und Berater. 8. aktualisierte und ergänzte Auflage.* Stuttgart, Zürich: Paul Haupt Verlag.

Haeske, U. (2003). *Konflikte im Arbeitsleben: Mit Mediation und Coaching zur Lösungsfindung.* München: Kösel-Verlag.

Hamilton, G. (2010). *Rapporteur Report: Alternative Dispute Resolution (ADR) - Definitions, Types and Feasibility.* Lexington: WLU - Washington and Lee University (School of Law).

Kals, E., & Ittner, H. (2008). *Wirtschaftsmediation.* Göttingen, Bern, Wien, u.a,: Hofgrefe Verlag.

König, E., & Volmer, G. (2008). *Handbuch Systemische Organisationsberatung.* Weinheim, Basel: Beltz Verlag.

Kurray, M. R. (2008). *Die Veränderung der Konfliktkultur durch Wirtschaftsmediation: Erfolgreiche Implementierung durch Change Management.* Hamburg: Diplomica-Verlag.

Rebmann, T. (o.J.). *Bundesverband Mediation > Was ist Mediation?* Abgerufen am 03. Juli 2011 von http://www.bmev.de/index.php?id=mediation

Selter, J. (2002). *Konfliktmanagement: Konflikte an der Hochschule: vorbeugen und kompetent bearbeiten.* Berlin: URL: http://www.hochschulkurs.de/fk1_2006_selter.pdf (Zugriff: 03.07.2011).

Tocholsky, K. (kein Datum). *StrauchMediation: Kommunikation für Wirtschaft & Politik.* Abgerufen am 02. Juli 2011 von http://www.strauch-mediation.de/index.php?option=com_content&view=article&id=48&Itemid=54

Troja, M., & Meuer, D. (2005). Mediation im öffentlichen Bereich. In G. Falk, P. Heintel, & E. E. Krainz, *Handbuch Mediation und Konfliktmanagement* (S. 219-242). Wiesbaden: VS Verlag.

Troja, M., & Meuer, D. (2005). Mediation im öffentlichen Bereich. In G. Falk, P. Heintel, & E. E. Krainz, *Handbuch Mediation und Konfliktmanagement* (S. 219-242). Wiesbaden: VS Verlag.

Vigenschow, U., Schneider, B., & Meyrose, I. (2010). *Soft Skills für Softwareentwickler: Fragetechniken, Konfliktmanagement, Kommunikationstypen und -modelle. 2., überarbeitete und erweiterte Auflage.* Heidelberg: dpunkt.verlag.

Weitz, T. T. (2008). *Gerichtsnahe Mediation in der Verwaltungs-, Sozial- und Finanzgerichtsbarkeit.* Frankfurt am Main: Peter Lang - Internationaler Verlag der Wissenschaften.

Weitz, T. T. (2008). *Gerichtsnahe Mediation in der Verwaltungs-, Sozial- und Finanzgerichtsbarkeit.* Frankfurt am Main: Peter Lang - Internationaler Verlag der Wissenschaften.

A 1905 Renault Park Phaeton owned by the Automobile Association since 1965. It was restored in 1954, having lain out of use between 1919 and 1952. The car has carried at least three different number plates in its lifetime – AA 1 was purchased in the 1960s from Winchester Council. The Association also owns AA 2 and AA 3.

Number Plates

A history of vehicle registration in Britain

Dave Moss

A Shire book

in association with the Michael Sedgwick Trust

Contents

Ancient history: the prologue 3

The golden age of motoring 5

The post-war years: changing times 9

Change, and change again: the arrival of computers 12

Modern times: a fresh start 15

Collectors' gold 21

Islands and Ireland 24

Curiosities and eccentricities, auctions and anomalies 27

Further reading 32

Acknowledgements 32

This work is published with the assistance of the Michael Sedgwick Trust. Founded in memory of the famous motoring researcher and author Michael Sedgwick (1926–83), the Trust is a Registered Charity to encourage the publishing of new research and recording of motoring history. Suggestions for future projects or donations should be sent to Hon. Sec. of the Michael Sedgwick Trust, c/o the National Motor Museum, Beaulieu, Hampshire SO42 7ZN, England.

British Library Cataloguing in Publication Data: Moss, Dave. Number plates: a history of vehicle registration in Britain. – (Shire album; 419) 1. Automobile licence plates – Great Britain – History I. Title 929.9 ISBN 0 7478 0566 0.

Front cover: *(Top) This Ormonde motorcycle was the first vehicle to be registered in Dorset and carried the controversial BF 1 plate until it left the county. Its new owner registered it in Somerset, where it gained the number Y 5. That mark was subsequently sold, so for modern road use it would carry an age-related number. The machine is seen here exhibited on loan at the Haynes Motor Museum at Sparkford in Somerset.*
(Bottom left) Years ago the pressures for favour of allocation of CAR 1 by Hertfordshire County Council must have been intense. This is surely one registration number that was not simply issued in the normal course of events. It has been owned by the Ford Motor Company for many years.
(Bottom right) More than a coincidence: a Volvo C70 convertible, with the car's manufacturer attempting to extract every ounce of publicity by purchasing for it a very suitable registration number.

Back cover: *The ready availability of 'off the shelf' registration numbers has brought a proliferation of manufacturer-owned vehicles carrying interesting plates. Volkswagen has adorned its Lupo with a plate that is about as close as it could be to the actual model name.*

Editorial Consultant: Michael E. Ware, former Director of the National Motor Museum, Beaulieu.

Published in 2006 by Shire Publications Ltd, Cromwell House, Church Street, Princes Risborough, Buckinghamshire HP27 9AA, UK. (Website: www.shirebooks.co.uk)
Copyright © 2003 by Dave Moss. First published 2003; reprinted 2006. Shire Album 419. ISBN-10: 0 7478 0566 0; ISBN-13: 978 0 7478 0566 3.
Dave Moss is hereby identified as the author of this work in accordance with Section 77 of the Copyright, Designs and Patents Act 1988.

Printed in Malta by Gutenberg Press Limited, Gudja Road, Tarxien PLA 19, Malta.

Ancient history: the prologue

Well before the principles of the internal combustion engine had been explored, steam was being considered as a source of power for road vehicles. In 1836, with Britain on the very brink of the railway age, a Parliamentary commission – neatly side-stepping the appalling state of Britain's roads at the time – reported itself 'definitely in favour of steam-powered road carriages'. The nineteenth-century public appeared rather less enthusiastic but took to the arrival of the railways with relish. For some time, the ease with which long-distance freight and passenger travel could be accomplished by rail diverted attention away from both the nightmare that was then Britain's road network and the severe practical difficulties involved in propelling heavy steam-powered vehicles even at low speeds along what were little more than cart tracks.

In 1861, the first Locomotive Acts limited the weight of road-going steam engines to 12 tons and imposed a speed limit of 10 mph (16 km/h). The railways began to prosper, while further legislation hindered and restricted the very notion of road vehicles. In 1865 another Locomotive Act reduced speed limits to 2 mph (3 km/h) in towns and 4 mph (6 km/h) in rural areas. However, the most onerous requirement, destined to enter the pages of history, was for a man to walk 60 yards (55 metres) in front of all powered vehicles, carrying a red flag or lantern. More than thirteen years then went by before the Locomotive (Amendment) Act of 1878 allowed authorities some discretion in imposing this requirement – and also reduced the separation distance between man and machine to a mere 20 yards (18 metres).

Another eighteen years passed before the Locomotives and Highways Act of 1896 swept away some – but not all – of these rules. Speed limits were raised to a heady 14 mph (23 km/h) and later reduced again, to 12 mph (19 km/h). Vehicle lighting and audible warning instruments became legal requirements, alongside rulings that vehicles must drive on the left and drivers must stop when requested by a police constable. These changes, and the removal of the red-flag rules for vehicles weighing under 3 tons, effectively laid the foundations for

Steam power was used on the roads before the internal combustion engine, and heavy vehicles were the first to require actual registration. This Foden steam lorry, christened 'Samantha', carries a late 1929 Buckinghamshire registration.

This 1897 chain-driven Daimler is older than Britain's registration system, introduced in 1904, at which time D 53 was allocated to this car by Kent County Council. Note the hyphen between the letter and the number – a feature that was eventually outlawed.

motoring as it has evolved today, paving the way for the arrival of smaller vehicles – especially those powered by the infant internal combustion engine.

With this Act came one other new requirement: all 'heavy locomotives' had to be licensed – and in some cases registered – by a relevant county council or county borough council. It was an innocuous move, but it was the first step towards the establishment of an enduring and comprehensive system of British vehicle registration and licensing.

The golden age of motoring

To celebrate the new-found freedom resulting from the Locomotives and Highways Act of 1896, the 'Motor Car Club' was established and organised an informal and celebratory drive from London to Brighton, which is still commemorated annually. The 1896 Act had introduced some basic regulations, yet the new breed of motorist, running a powered vehicle on two, three or four wheels, could effectively do whatever he or she wished, since such vehicles were virtually untraceable. At that time only large road vehicles had to be registered or licensed – and, amongst other things, the Motor Car Act of 1903 sought to address this anomaly by requiring motor-vehicle drivers to be licensed every year.

Yet the 1903 Act is more notable as the instrument that brought wide-ranging vehicle registration and licensing schemes to Britain for the first time. An important new requirement was for all vehicles to display a registration 'mark', allowing them to be easily traced. There was also an increased speed limit, of 20 mph (32 km/h), and another new concept: fines, for the driving of unlicensed vehicles, for general speeding, and for 'reckless driving' – a new offence. County councils and county borough councils were appointed as the authorities responsible for the new registration and licensing schemes, with fees set at 20 shillings for a vehicle registration and 5 shillings for a driver's licence.

Responding to the Act of 1903, a now long-forgotten Westminster civil servant came up with a straightforward, easily recognisable system of vehicle registration marks – which

Since the start of the new registration-mark system in 2001, the dimensions, font and actual manufacture of plates has been tightly controlled. Not so in the 1930s, when long-established accessory maker Bluemels advertised the opportunity for anyone to make or modify a six-figure number plate – at prices starting from 7s 3d.

Above left: *This Swift from 1919 appears at first glance to be carrying an authentic registration – but all is not what it seems... Swift collapsed in 1931, and Glass's invaluable 'Index to Motor Vehicle Registration Numbers for 1935' reveals that Kinross County Council, which then issued SV allocations, had reached only SV 1034 by January 1935.*

Above right: *The Fordson 7V flatbed lorry to which this FRU 256 registration belongs was first registered in Bournemouth in 1944. It was found in a barn in 2002 – where it had stood since falling out of use in 1965.*

developed into one of the most enduring features of the entire age of motoring in the British Isles. The new alphabet-based system included a regional identification plan, founded on the then national arrangement of county councils and county borough councils (burgh councils in Scotland). Early registration marks consisted of single letters and up to four numbers, the letters representing strategically placed urban or rural councils in descending order of total population around the British Isles. Under this system, the first registration mark to be allocated was A 1, issued by London County Council soon after the 1903 legislation received royal assent. Some letters – G, I, S, V and Z – were earmarked for use in Scotland and Ireland, and, along with Q, were withheld. The remaining twenty letters were insufficient to provide all English authorities with registration allocations, so (with some exceptions, particularly combinations that included letters from the list above as 'second' letters) two-letter combinations starting at AA and proceeding as far as FP were also issued.

The remaining two-letter combinations were then allocated over a period of time, with most (but by no means all) being brought into use before 1920. In some areas, where a high demand was anticipated, multiple allocations of often consecutive pairs of letters were made, and there were also attempts to make some marks identifiable with the specific area from which they came – such as DV for Devon, and several others. Rural counties and remote areas frequently received only single allocations.

The Roads Act of 1920 consolidated and further formalised vehicle registration marks in Britain and also removed some interesting anomalies. Until 1920, authorities had not been prevented from keeping separate registers for both cars and motorcycles – so it was possible, and not unknown, to find a car and a motorcycle with the same registration mark. Some counties used 'leading zeros' on two-wheeler registrations as a method of differentiation. Also, before 1920, marks could be reused: if a vehicle left a council's area it would lose its registration, gaining a new one elsewhere. The mark thus released would then be used again – on a completely different vehicle.

New allocations appeared over quite a long period. During 1931, for instance,

A Morris Cowley, first registered in Surrey early in 1930. Note the lettered stop light – hardly a high-visibility item – and the Bluemels Model 'C' number plate with single rear light as in the advertisement illustrated on page 5.

This Thurgood-bodied thirty-five-seater half-cab coach, seen awaiting restoration, was originally registered in Northampton-shire in 1931. Its registration number continues in use – by the son of the coach's original owner. The vehicle itself now has an age-related mark: PSL 234.

Three ages of Vauxhall, each with a different type of number plate: the Denbigh-registered H type 'Ten' (left) carries a typical early pressed-aluminium plate; the 1966 Yorkshire-registered Viva SL (centre) has a plate using separately attached, silver-painted plastic characters; and the 1961 F type Victor has a smooth perspex plate – an ancestor of the reflective types used since 1973.

Old vehicles continue to turn up after long periods of inactivity – still, remarkably, in restorable condition. This semi-complete Austin 7 carries its original registration mark, issued by Southampton Borough Council early in 1933.

Right: *This Bean commercial is one of the few survivors of a model that was rare even when in production. It was registered in Warwick early in 1931, a couple of months before the Bean company was put into receivership.*

Northamptonshire was just starting to issue NV marks with one or two numbers, NV 9240 not being issued until 1937. Yet, in contrast, authorities in areas with high registration demands – Middlesex and Staffordshire, for example – were already on the point of exhausting their allocated combinations of one or two letters plus four digits. So, by mid 1932, Staffordshire was already introducing its first plates of three letters and up to three digits, which became the backbone of the registration system until the mid 1950s. In such registrations the second and third letters provided the established area identification, while the additional first letter (with I, Q and Z not used) provided councils with nearly 23,000 extra marks for each area identifier under their control.

After the introduction of this new arrangement – three letters followed by up to three numbers – in the 1930s, the number-plate system entered a period of stability. Ever-growing vehicle sales following the Second World War prompted the next change, when some authorities simply came to the end of all their available three-letter/three-number allocations. Further combinations were made available by 'reversing' the order of marks available for issue, putting up to four numbers ahead of one or two letters, or up to three numbers ahead of three letters. This theoretically gave issuing authorities the same number of 'reversed' combinations as had already been allocated in the original format – the plates once again carrying the now long-established area identifiers in the single, or second and third, alphabetical characters.

The post-war years: changing times

Throughout the 1950s, car and motorcycle sales increased inexorably – with both issuing authorities and the Government gradually realising that the fifty-year-old vehicle registration system was approaching the end of a lengthy road. The advent of 'numbers first, letters last' combinations, first issued by Middlesex in 1953, marked the start of a period during which some authorities worked through their available allocations with alarming speed. By this time, vehicle sales growth was such that the system – which had lasted in many cases fifty years or more in its original guise – was all but exhausted by some authorities in around ten years when the format was reversed!

Between 1953 and 1963, five- and six-character 'reversed' plates became commonplace, with some authorities (where such marks were allocated many years earlier) using allocations comprising four digits followed by single-letter identifiers. The use of 'reversed' single-letter allocations invariably indicated a pressing shortage of available registration combinations for the authority concerned. Single-letter allocations known to have been issued in 'reversed' format before 1965 include D (briefly in 1964), E, F (in two stages), H, K, N, R, U, W and Z. Some other low-number, single-letter reversed combinations were allocated for trade-plate

The humble Austin delivery van was once a common sight. This example dates from 1958 – the year Devon started on its 'reversed' number-plate sequences. The old commercial 'C' licence displayed in the windscreen expired in 1965.

9

An immaculately presented MGA fixed-head coupé, first registered on 9th October 1957. Sensitive observers will spot that it carries an age-related registration, having lost its original Cambridge-issued mark, SCE 280, in the 1990s.

sequences, and there is circumstantial evidence that the same 'single-letter' numbers were occasionally used for both normal and trade-plate allocations.

In the days long before sales of specific registration marks were contemplated, or any status or financial value was attached to them, all available letters and numbers in a sequence from 1 to 999 were usually issued. Unless buyers could 'pull rank' or had a contact in the right office at the licensing authority – far from unknown, particularly with the bigger dealers – until well into the 1960s vehicle buyers simply took pot luck on their new registration number. After 1983, low numbers (invariably below 20, and often up to 100) were not generally issued, being held back for outright sale by the DVLA. Yet the system that operated until the 1960s on the basis of 'Here's the next number in line, take it or leave it' led – surreptitious backhanders apart – to the numbers 1 to 100 being a more common sight on the roads than has been the case since 1983.

By 1960 there were wide variations in the rate at which authorities were registering vehicles. In sharp contrast to the pressures of demand in the urban areas, registrations proceeded much more slowly away from major population centres. In Scotland and Ireland, 1960s allocations were still being made from the 'two letters followed by four numbers' series, first issued in 1904. By the time suffix letters were introduced in 1963–4, Bute (SJ) was still registering

The Ford V8 Pilot was produced for a limited period, ending early in the 1950s. This well-preserved example was registered by Middlesex Council, one of several counties perpetually short of registration marks. Late in 1953 Middlesex became the first authority to issue 'reversed' sequences.

From a series built for less than two years, this Tickford-bodied Land-Rover was one of the last of its type, registered by Glamorgan County Council in 1950. Since the estate bodywork attracted British purchase tax, most were exported – and very few survive.

vehicles in the SJ 2800 range and never actually issued any three-letter/three-number combinations.

These varying circumstances meant that, as the 1960s approached, British roads were alive with a more diverse selection of registration marks than at any time during the previous fifty years. Perhaps that is why the 1950s and 1960s were the golden age of the schoolboy number-plate collecting craze.

Though there was little outward sign, by the early 1960s it was becoming an increasing Government priority to find alternative ways of dealing with vehicle registration and ownership procedures. Slowly but surely the amount of paperwork – and its movement around the country – was gradually overwhelming the system's ability to cope. In 1960 alone, over 820,000 new cars were sold in Britain, adding to those already on the roads – yet vehicle registration administration was still based on manual systems established almost sixty years earlier. Another problem was the lack of direct, automatic correlation of vehicle and driver records between autonomous areas. Routine police requests to check vehicle records were labour intensive and time-consuming, which in turn made fraudulent activities relatively easy.

Until the distinct trend towards lower, wider body styles emerged in the post-war years, upright bodywork lent itself aesthetically to rectangular number plates such as this, carried on a 1938 Vauxhall H type 'Ten'. Since the 1970s, aside from some commercials, motorcycles and specialist vehicles, rectangular number plates have become much less common.

The public was also starting to suffer, as delays within the registration and licensing system lengthened. Yet, aside from these growing administrative problems, as we have seen, there was another major issue. Some authorities were facing a shortage of vehicle registration marks as the last of their available 'reversed' allocations appeared on the horizon. By 1960, major changes to Britain's driver and vehicle registration systems were not just inevitable – but looming large.

Change, and change again:
the arrival of computers

At the start of the 1960s, Britain's registration mark system was under review. In sixty years the only major change had been a move to 'reversed' plates, but by 1963 all obvious possibilities of the original system had been exhausted. Consultation was undertaken with the police and the motor trade, after which officialdom decided to add a new 'suffix' letter at the end of the plate as a year identifier.

The opportunity was also taken to revert to the principle of letters first, numbers last in order to avoid confusion with the immediately preceding issue of non-suffix plates – and the new system brought some very useful benefits. For the first time, it was possible for anyone interested to quickly date a vehicle to within twelve months – and the new system also neatly overcame the inherent volume limitations imposed by a registration mark's previous six-character format. Influenced by the earlier system, the new plates featured three letters, with the second and third still indicating the issuing area, plus up to three numbers – all followed by an 'A' suffix, denoting 1963 as the year of registration. Following tradition, neither the first letter nor the suffix could be I, Q or Z, but all numbers up to 999 could be allocated. The

A summer Saturday on the notorious Exeter bypass in 1963 – with no sign of a brand-new 'A' suffix registration. The AA motorcycle is London registered, the broken-down Triumph is from Somerset, whilst the Vauxhall Victor with caravan is from Sheffield, and the Triumph Herald hails from Lancashire. Such lengthy journeys must have taken considerable time in 1963 with so few motorways – but at least there was no speed limit away from the towns!

Spot the impostor ... One of this trio of interesting British products carries a non-original registration. The J-registered Morris Oxford on the left was definitely one of the last before the new Marina arrived, and the MG Midget also appears genuine. But the very early 1962 Riley Elf has unfortunately lost its original registration, carrying a rather obvious age-related mark.

added suffix letter allowed many more registration combinations – effectively all those available with each two-letter allocation possessed by each authority, preceded by all available letters of the alphabet – with all such possible combinations being usable in a period of just twelve months. Then, by adding the next alphabetical suffix letter for the following year, precisely the same number of possible combinations was available again, every single year, for at least twenty years to come.

Enacted by some authorities in England, Scotland and Wales for vehicles registered on or after 1st January 1963, the new marks first appeared in areas hard pressed for available registrations. Interestingly, the new suffix system seems to have coincided with some authorities' treatment of numbers below 100 as rather special. About this time, realisation seems to have dawned that some combinations of available letters and numbers might have a value beyond that of simple vehicle registration. Some (but by no means all) authorities started their suffix-type allocations with the number 1 – though from 1963, low numbers seemed to turn up far more frequently than logic would suggest on vehicles such as tractors, trucks, buses and mopeds. The implication is that this was a deliberate policy, since private car registrations in 1963 considerably outweighed those of all other vehicles – so cars ought to have had more low-number allocations.

The new system had clear practical advantages, though not all authorities used it immediately. Quite a few areas did not issue any 'A' suffix plates, and more than a handful did not issue any 'B' suffixes either, but by 1965, under Government exhortation, all authorities were using the new scheme. Many authorities never exhausted their stock of six-character allocations, which was perhaps fortunate, since they were to prove useful many years later!

There were 1,148,718 new cars sold in 1965, and many more changed hands – and owners and drivers of course continued to change addresses. Driver and vehicle registration records were still being updated manually by councils, and existing handling systems were indisputably overwhelmed. A complete breakdown of the licensing system was averted in the

13

The stylish Borgward Isabella Coupé was always a rarity. This example was registered in Surrey, one of several authorities always short of registration allocations – hence the 'reversed' four-figure, two-letter registration mark, issued in 1960.

nick of time with the establishment of the new Driver and Vehicle Licensing Centre (DVLC) in Swansea in 1965.

The DVLC, with its centralised systems, brought benefits in the faster processing of driving-licence changes, but did not immediately become a centre for the administration of vehicle registration marks. That required a common, centrally based registration system – achievable only by transferring huge amounts of vehicle data, until then held by local and county councils, on to a new computer record. The belated move in 1965 requiring authorities to use the annual suffix-letter arrangement was the first step in that direction. However, actually implementing a computer-based vehicle registration system took far longer than was anticipated – and left a legacy that vehicle enthusiasts and historians alike have come to regret.

Modern times: a fresh start

In 1967, largely at the behest of the manufacturers and retailers of private cars, the start of the new registration year was changed from 1st January to 1st August. The intention was to move the peak of new-car sales activity from Christmas and the New Year to the summer,

when, the theory went, fewer people would want to buy new vehicles. It did not turn out like that, but the change nevertheless became permanent, running for thirty-two years until 1999. This led to the 'E' suffix becoming the first real oddity in the new system, used only for the first seven months of 1967.

Some years later, legislation significantly altered the appearance of British number plates for the first time in seventy years. Government had tinkered with the dimensions, spacing and layout of characters on number plates on several occasions since 1903, but a dramatic change occurred on 1st January 1973. Newly registered vehicles were required to have 'reflective style' number plates, with black letters on a white background at the front, and on a yellow background at the rear. Older style plates, with white or silver letters on a black background, remained legal for vehicles already registered.

Then, in 1974, after nine years of seemingly endless delay, the DVLC was finally able to administer new vehicle registrations centrally – in practice via its Local Vehicle Licensing Offices. In October of that year, formal responsibility for the

The first significant anomaly of the suffix-based registration system came in 1967. In that year, the suffix change moved to August, so the 'E' suffix lasted only seven months. As a result, 'E' suffixes are a relative rarity – especially on open-top AEC Regent double-deck buses!

Vehicle manufacturers' publicity material often throws up anomalies. Aside from one or two diplomatic vehicles, three-letter plates starting with Q have never been issued in Britain. Why the then brand-new V8 MGBGT in this 1975 British Leyland publicity shot has one is unknown.

The long-established black-and-white number plate was outlawed by legislation that required reflective front and rear plates to be used for vehicles registered after 1st January 1973. This K-registered, late-1972 V12 E type Jaguar was therefore one of the last vehicles to take to British roads with the old-style plates.

issue of vehicle registration marks passed to the DVLC from local councils, coinciding – perhaps unfortunately – with a time of major reorganisation of local government. From 1974, the waters of the established vehicle registration system became muddied, as new boundaries, the new centralised structure and continued growth in vehicle numbers forced the reassignment of many long-established area codes to improve the efficiency of registration-mark usage.

Many marks then came to represent newly defined and occasionally completely different licensing areas, whilst others were gradually withdrawn from use. For many years the Local Vehicle Licensing Office network remained quite faithful to the original system, even though further complications arose as the number of local offices – now called Vehicle Registration Offices – continued to shrink. Then, following the introduction of 'automated first registration', the eighty original offices were reduced to around forty. This brought yet further

Daihatsu was the first Japanese car manufacturer to set up a British sales network. This is its 1964 Compagno Berlina model, with styling apparently borrowed from contemporary 1960s Fiat models. In 1964, its registration was probably allocated on a 'next in line' basis, with no monetary significance. The passage of time has since made it quite valuable.

16

changes to both regional identities and the range of marks allocated.

Once the centralised process of registering new vehicles had started, the DVLC set about the huge task of converting existing vehicles' old, and increasingly fraud-prone, three-way folding log-books into less characterful, computer-generated slips of paper denoting ownership. To enter each individual vehicle's data on to the computer, owners' log-books had to be sent to the DVLC. On request, the original (often well-worn) log-book could be returned afterwards, but only the most dedicated owners seem to have asked for this, so relatively few such log-books (known as the 'V60') now exist. Fewer still remain with the vehicle to which they truly belong.

By 1983, as the 'Y' suffix letter changed to an 'A' prefix – doubling the life of the system, just as had happened thirty years earlier – the records of all licensed vehicles registered in England, Scotland and Wales had been entered on to Swansea's computers. Many other vehicles still existed that, for a variety of reasons, were not at that time licensed for road use. During 1983, advertisements were placed, and vehicle clubs contacted, encouraging owners to preserve existing registration marks by registering them on the Swansea computers. Around 200,000 'not-in-use' vehicles were notified to the DVLC before the vehicle record was finally 'closed' on 30th November 1983. This closure was to become a bone of contention and a source of difficulty for historic-vehicle owners for years to come, though for

This Devon registration was issued in 1983 – before plates featuring the number 666 stopped appearing in the normal run of events. Although the vehicle is of a certain age, the plate features the latest font, introduced for new vehicles in September 2001, and at the same time becoming mandatory for replacement number plates on all vehicles dating back to 1973.

This 1970/71 Monmouth-registered pickup was based on the popular A60/Morris Oxford passenger cars, whose design roots lay in the 1950s. Though rare even in its heyday, its structural relationship to the commercial van is revealed by the alternative, lower number-plate position. Like the earliest Minis, the opening tailgate included a hinged number-plate bracket, allowing carriage of long loads. Such use can hardly have helped the visibility of rear lights and indicators for following traffic, especially at night.

most vehicle users and owners it led to another period of registration-number stability.

Ever-increasing new-car sales and the limitation of a twenty-one-letter usable alphabet (excluding I, O, U, Q and Z) effectively spelled a twenty-year maximum lifespan for the 'prefix-style' registration system that commenced in 1983. Several options for the best way forward were reviewed by Government, and consultations opened midway through the 1990s. The responses indicated that, to cope with rising vehicle-registration volumes and to aid policing as far as possible, a new system was necessary – bringing Britain's original, time-honoured registration system to an end. Twice-yearly prefix-letter changes, enacted in 1999 – with the 'change months' becoming March and September – brought forward the demise of

Local Memory Tags

Letter		Local Office	DVLA Local Office Identifier
A	Anglia	Peterborough Norwich Ipswich	AA AB AC AD AE AF AG AH AJ AK AL AM AN AO AP AR AS AT AU AV AW AX AY
B	Birmingham	Birmingham	BA – BY
C	Cymru	Cardiff Swansea Bangor	CA CB CC CD CE CF CG CH CJ CK CL CM CN CO CP CR CS CT CU CV CW CX CY
D	Deeside to Shrewsbury	Chester Shrewsbury	DA DB DC DD DE DF DG DH DJ DK DL DM DN DO DP DR DS DT DU DV DW DX DY
E	Essex	Chelmsford	EA – EY
F	Forest & Fens	Nottingham Lincoln	FA FB FC FD FE FF FG FH FJ FK FL FM FN FP FR FS FT FV FW FX FY
G	Garden of England	Maidstone Brighton	GA GB GC GD GE GF GG GH GJ GK GL GM GN GO GP GR GS GT GU GV GW GX GY
H	Hampshire & Dorset	Bournemouth Portsmouth	HA HB HC HD HE HF HG HH HJ HK HL HM HN HO HP HR HS HT HU HV HW HX HY (HW will be used exclusively for Isle of Wight residents)
K		Luton Northampton	KA KB KC KD KE KF KG KH KJ KK KL KM KN KO KP KR KS KT KU KV KW KX KY
L	London	Wimbledon Stanmore Sidcup	LA LB LC LD LE LF LG LH LJ LK LL LM LN LO LP LR LS LT LU LV LW LX LY
M	Manchester & Merseyside	Manchester	MA – MY
N	North	Newcastle Stockton	NA NB NC ND NE NG NH NJ NK NL NM NN NO NP NR NS NT NU NV NW NX NY
O	Oxford	Oxford	OA – OY
P	Preston	Preston Carlisle	PA PB PC PD PE PF PG PH PJ PK PL PM PN PO PP PR PS PT PU PV PW PX PY
R	Reading	Reading	RA – RY
S	Scotland	Glasgow Edinburgh Dundee Aberdeen Inverness	SA SB SC SD SE SF SG SH SJ SK SL SM SN SO SP SR SS ST SU SV SW SX SY
V	Severn Valley	Worcester	VA – VY
W	West of England	Exeter Truro Bristol	WA WB WC WD WE WF WG WH WJ WK WL WM WN WO WP WR WS WT WU WV WW WX WY
Y	Yorkshire	Leeds Sheffield Beverley	YA YB YC YD YE YF YG YH YJ YK YL YM YN YO YP YR YS YT YU YV YW YX YY

NB: DVLA cannot guarantee that any specific local memory tag or DVLA Local Office Identifier will be issued.

Age identifiers

Date	Code	Date	Code
		Sept 2001 – Feb 2002	51
March 2002 – Aug 2002	02	Sept 2002 – Feb 2003	52
March 2003 – Aug 2003	03	Sept 2003 – Feb 2004	53
March 2004 – Aug 2004	04	Sept 2004 – Feb 2005	54
March 2005 – Aug 2005	05	Sept 2005 – Feb 2006	55
March 2006 – Aug 2006	06	Sept 2006 – Feb 2007	56
March 2007 – Aug 2007	07	Sept 2007 – Feb 2008	57
March 2008 – Aug 2008	08	Sept 2008 – Feb 2009	58
March 2009 – Aug 2009	09	Sept 2009 – Feb 2010	59
March 2010 – Aug 2010	10	Sept 2010 – Feb 2011	60
March 2011 – Aug 2011	11	Sept 2011 – Feb 2012	61

This pattern will continue until all permutations are exhausted.

Further information about number plates can be obtained by:

Telephoning DVLA Vehicle Enquiries on **0870 240 0010**

Customers with impaired hearing who have a textphone/minicom should phone 01792 782756 for vehicle enquiries.

You should be aware that the minincom number will **not** respond to ordinary telephones.

Fax: **01792 782793**,

DVLA website **http://www.dvla.gov.uk**

E-mail at **vehicles.dvla@gtnet.gov.uk**

An (almost) complete list of 'new' area identifiers, as issued by the DVLA in 2001. This is built around regional Vehicle Registration Office locations, providing a useful indication of where post-2001 vehicles were first registered. X identifiers are not shown but are issued for VAT-free vehicle sales.

The September 2001 number-plate system has led to various new sought-after numbers being sold through the DVLA Select Registrations scheme. Here, plates are being assembled to promote new-number sales, though the mark shown appears to be a valid Birmingham registration, available for issue in the six months commencing March 2002.

the old system. The final 'Y'-prefix plates were issued on 31st August 2001.

The brand-new registration system introduced the following day created some press interest but was hardly an issue for most motorists. Yet the new arrangement was completely different, designed to cope with registration volumes such that the designers of the earlier system could hardly have imagined. The numeric basis of the original was replaced by an alphabetic foundation in the new system. Two letters – unrelated to the earlier area codes – indicate, first, the issuing region and, second, the issuing office. These are followed by two numbers, indicating the month and year of issue. The plates are then completed by three randomly selected letters, excluding only I and Q.

Some 13,824 registration combinations are therefore possible for each issuing-office prefix,

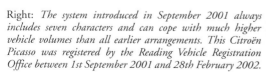

Left: *From 1974, and particularly since 1989, genuine Scottish registrations became rarer as the number of issuing offices declined and fewer of the many earlier unique Scottish combinations were issued. This 1991–2 J-plated Rover diesel hails from Edinburgh, which in the post-2001 system uses SK, SL, SM, SN and SO codes – none of which belonged to Edinburgh in earlier times.*

Right: *The system introduced in September 2001 always includes seven characters and can cope with much higher vehicle volumes than all earlier arrangements. This Citroën Picasso was registered by the Reading Vehicle Registration Office between 1st September 2001 and 28th February 2002.*

These three manufacturer-owned Vauxhalls were all registered in the company's home town of Luton. The Corsa and Astra coupé with 02 identifiers took to the road in the six months commencing March 2002, whilst the Astra LS ECO4 diesel on the right is newer, entering service after September 2002.

so in this system volumes can be huge. Taking the Truro registration office as an example, two prefix allocations, WK and WL, are available – allowing the issue of 27,648 of the 331,776 possible West of England registrations in the series WA–WY (excluding I and Q) in every licensing period. This system was introduced with plate changes every six months, but more changes per year are perfectly possible.

With twice-yearly plate changes and nineteen DVLA regions, designated A–Y (excluding I, J, Q, T, U, X – for VAT-free sales – and Z), the maximum number of vehicles that could be registered nationally each year is over 12.6 million. With monthly plate changes, some 75.6 million registrations each year could be accommodated! The considerable amount of reserve capacity available can be appreciated by comparing this potential annual registration figure with the all-time record new-car sales of 2001, which reached 2.46 million units. Furthermore, this new system will not be exhausted until 2049, when 'reversed' plates might once again be used, thus immediately extending the system's life by another forty-eight years.

Only time will tell whether registration marks now being issued will have a similar resilience for survival or the following amongst schoolboys with notebooks that their illustrious predecessors enjoyed in their heyday ... And who knows what vehicles might be in use when the current British number-plate system finally runs out of road in 2097 – 195 years after British cars first displayed registration numbers?

Collectors' gold

As closure of the vehicle record loomed, a booming trade in number-plate 'sales' and 'transfers' sprang up, as those looking to make money rediscovered old or derelict vehicles with number plates whose value might potentially far outweigh that of the vehicle itself. Some of the marks that emerged, combining very low numbers and perhaps one, two or three letters, reached back to the dawn of motoring, begging questions about whether all resulting applications for registration-mark transfers were entirely legitimate.

The intrinsic historical value of donor vehicles carrying such registrations was rarely considered in this process. Rarity or originality of the vehicle and the possibility of its restoration were all too often not a real concern for those wanting a quick and easy source of income. Desirable early plates were either hastily transferred to other vehicles or held by use of a 'retention certificate'. Many still restorable vehicles lost their original registration numbers in this period as opportunists scoured the countryside seeking quick and very occasionally major financial gain. The more unscrupulous explored all the possible avenues – up to and including the complete and bogus recreation of numbers no longer extant.

After closure of the vehicle record in November 1983, vehicles not logged on DVLC computers could reclaim their original mark only via a tortuous process, requiring substantive evidence that the vehicle was especially rare or of historical significance. This usually proved quite difficult because, in the centralisation of records between 1974 and 1983, very large amounts (but thankfully not all) of the unique paper-based vehicle registration data, painstakingly compiled over many years by county and borough councils, was lost or destroyed. Though some manual records survive in various archives, those for many urban areas have been lost forever.

Without such records, enthusiasts soon found that demonstrating rarity or historical significance – even direct provenance to a registration number still carried by a vehicle –

The last Triumph sports car officially on sale in Britain was the unloved TR7. Enthusiasts said it needed more power, and British Leyland eventually shoehorned in the Rover V8 engine – but the resulting TR8 was for export only. Just a few factory-built V8 cars were sold in Britain before all versions were discontinued. This is one of the last four hundred TR8s, built in 1981.

could be an enormous task. Under the new, tightly drawn regulations, vehicles returning to use after 1983, if no right to use an original mark could be directly proven, were issued with a so-called 'age-related' registration. This system, still operating in modified form, broadly allows the DVLA (as it is now) to issue a mark that at least looks as if it has come from the period in which the vehicle first entered service.

Following closure of the record, it gradually became clear that the classic-vehicle movement was far from convinced by the re-registration arrangements that had been introduced. Mounting concern was expressed through owners' clubs by numbers of increasingly vociferous members as it became clear that old vehicles that, for whatever reason, had not been recorded on the DVLA computers by November 1983 would never again be able to bear their original registration mark. Eventually the Federation of British Historic Vehicle Clubs (FBHVC) formally approached the DVLA on behalf of the classic-vehicle movement, pointing out that this was a serious, sizeable and ongoing problem, which questioned vehicle authenticity simply because original registration marks could no longer be used.

This left-hand-drive 1960 Commer Karrier mobile home is an unlikely resting place for a 1923-allocated Glasgow registration – but that does not make the plate any less valuable! Its counterpart, 32 GB, was sold for £6200 in a DVLA registration-numbers auction in 2002.

Not many cars can claim a number plate that is also their model name. This 1998 Nissan Micra is one of the few, sporting a valuable plate owned by Nissan Motor GB Ltd.

A lengthy period of negotiation followed, until finally, after seven years of wrangling between the authorities and a range of owners' clubs and prominent individuals, co-ordinated and spearheaded by the FBHVC, the DVLA caved in to increasing pressure. From 1990, subject to verification, the reassignment of known original registration marks was allowed, on a 'non-transferable' basis. Such non-transferability, agreed with the Federation, was designed to prevent false claims arising for old numbers – since there can be no ongoing cash value in an old vehicle's registration number (no matter how desirable) if it is not transferable.

Though still not perfect, the modified 'age-related' system introduced after negotiation has stood the test of time. Reappearing vehicles that can be dated to before 1931 receive a two-letter, four-digit combination, from incomplete, previously unissued sequences. Vehicles that can be accurately dated between 1931 and 1963 are likely to receive a three-letter, three-digit mark, usually using combinations originally allocated to remote Scottish authorities – these are the only series where significant quantities of such unissued marks remain. For a while, vehicles dated between 1956 and 1963 were occasionally provided with marks from unissued sequences with an 'A' suffix – not, of course, originally issued before 1963. The DVLA has recognised that this system again challenges authenticity, and now issues more appropriate age-related marks wherever possible. Post-1963 vehicles get a suitable unissued plate with the relevant year suffix (or prefix). If the age of a vehicle is uncertain – a particular problem with imported and kit cars – 'Q' suffixes or prefixes are allocated.

This rare 1939 German Schlüter tractor was a post-war import, intended only for off-road agricultural use when it arrived in Britain. As such it was not road-registered at the time. Since 1980, in the absence of substantive evidence of previous registration, the only possible way any vehicle such as this can now legally be used on British roads is via an (often less than authentic) age-related number plate – as seen here.

In both the old and new systems, the Isle of Wight has its own unique registration identification. This 1972 Rover 3.5 litre coupé, photographed in 2001, carries its 1973–4 Isle of Wight DL registration plate with pride – it is one of the lucky coupés of the period, since most of the small volume produced have succumbed to terminal rust.

Islands and Ireland

The Isle of Wight

For many years the Isle of Wight, with county council status, used the area letters DL within the general system for all vehicle registrations. Following gradual rationalisation of DVLA local offices, DL identifiers were issued by Portsmouth Vehicle Registration Office. Under the system that started on 1st September 2001, the island falls within the Hampshire and Dorset region, and HW is used exclusively for residents of the island.

The Isle of Man

The Isle of Man introduced vehicle registration soon after Britain, in the same format, with the first MN registrations, having up to four digits, issued in 1906. This series endured for some time, before the island moved on to a three-letter, three-digit sequence commencing with AMN. The MAN series was also used, diverted from West Ham Borough Council, where it was made unavailable. The letters MAN followed by four digits have also been used. All these series have also been issued in reverse. The island did not follow the British 'year identifier' system introduced in 1963, though since then its plates have utilised both suffix and prefix letters as integral parts of the registration, on a seven-character plate of British appearance.

Guernsey and Jersey

Vehicles here have carried mandatory registration marks since before 1915, with each island having a unique arrangement not related to the British registration system. Guernsey vehicles carry a straightforward numerical plate with no letters and, in 2003, up to five figures. Jersey also uses a five-figure series, preceded by the single letter J. Interestingly, J was also allocated by the mainland county of Durham, between 1903 and 1922.

For many years, Guernsey plates have been issued in a numerical sequence without age identifiers. The lower the number, the longer the plate has been around – but this is no indication of vehicle age, which can be disguised by number transfers. The author spotted the single number 5 in use on a modern vehicle in Pembrokeshire in 2002.

Right: *Jersey follows a similar numerical progression to Guernsey – except that its registration plates are preceded by the single letter J.*

The Isles of Scilly

The registration mark SCY (with suffixes and, later, prefixes) was made available for use on these islands in 1971, and simultaneously withdrawn from use by Swansea – which had previously issued that combination. Because there are relatively few vehicles on the Isles of Scilly, any plate carrying the registration SCY is a rare sight on the mainland.

Ireland

The legislation bringing Britain's registration mark system into use in 1904, as consolidated and modified by the Roads Act of 1920, was also effective in Ireland. Provisions within the Acts that introduced separation in 1921 ensured that existing British legislation was binding until later amendment – and the still relatively new British registration system therefore prevailed both north and south of the new Irish border.

Initially the thirty-two Irish counties were allocated thirty-three two-letter combinations in alphabetical order. These ran from IA to IZ, followed by AI, BI etc, but excluding the letters S, V and G (all initially reserved for Scotland), as well as Q and the rather confusing II. Thirty-three marks were issued because Tipperary received separate allocations for its north (FI) and south (HI) ridings. Before Irish separation in 1922, King's County was allocated the letters IR.

With later Northern Ireland plates carrying no year-identifier letters, owners modest about their vehicle's age have discovered that such registrations can be used to hide it. NDZ 6342 was originally issued by Ballymena between October 1992 and April 1993. This Nissan, however, is much newer than that.

Northern Irish registrations are popular with coach operators. Only an expert would know the age of this coach, which carries an Omagh plate issued between December 1999 and October 2000.

Afterwards it was known as Offaly, though the IR allocation remained – resulting in a break in the original, neat IA to IZ alphabetical county sequence. Similarly, Laois (CI) was originally known as Queen's County. County Wicklow's NI was the last allocation in this series, after which the major Irish cities took OI to WI – and, later, XI, YI and ZI. Eventually, a registration shortage affected the less rural parts of Ireland, just as it had in Britain. This resulted in the allocation of some two-letter Z combinations, with the Irish Free State using Z and ZA–ZY, and Northern Ireland AZ–YZ. From the end of the 1950s, as areas used up their two-letter, four-figure series, three-letter, three-figure combinations were introduced, similar to those in Great Britain. Elsewhere, two-letter, four-figure combinations continued, with the very last issued by Leitrim County Council (IT) in 1972.

In 1966 the Northern Ireland system was changed, though the year suffix and prefix system adopted in Britain was not used. Instead, a three-letter, four-digit system was introduced, with area identification carried by the second and third letters – always including an I or a Z. The number of area codes on issue diminished somewhat following early-1970s legislation that gave control of vehicle registration to the Northern Ireland Government.

Though the Irish Free State subsequently became Eire, and later the Republic of Ireland, the registration-mark system set up before the Act of Separation remained in use until January 1987, when a new scheme was introduced. The mainland year prefix and suffix system was not used, though the new arrangements still featured a year identifier. This is represented by the first two digits on an eight-character (maximum) plate, followed by one or two letters, in turn followed by up to five digits. The letters are area identifiers – but from a new sequence, bearing no relation to the old, mainland-based, I and Z system.

Curiosities and eccentricities, auctions and anomalies

Trade plates

The 1903 legislation provided a framework for temporary 'custody rather than ownership' situations. This foresaw circumstances in which vehicles were being repaired, loaned or demonstrated to customers by the motor trade or others, and allowed temporary public road use. Two distinct types of so-called 'general identification plate' were provided for: 'general' plates had a red background with white lettering, whilst 'limited' plates were the reverse of this. Only one type remained in 2003, universally known as the 'trade' plate, having a creamy white background with red lettering. Though a new general registration system was introduced in September 2001, trade plates continue to use the earlier system, with up to three digits, followed by one or two letters from the original area-identifier list. Interestingly, though not uniquely, trade-plate numbers in the 1 to 99 range are preceded by one or two leading zeros. Early in the twentieth century, when cars and motorcycles could carry the same registration, motorcycle numbers up to 99 sometimes also carried leading zeros. At the start of the twenty-first century, just a handful of such marks remained on the DVLA database.

Temporary imports, permanent exports and VAT

The first arrangements to formalise the international transfer of motor vehicles were introduced before the First World War, and in mainland Britain these brought the introduction of QQ registrations. With London as the issuing authority, these (and

A very few authorities issued 'zero' registration marks – sometimes long after the original start of a one- or two-letter series at number 1. LM 0 is the Lord Mayor of the City of London's car, but others known to have been issued include G 0 and S 0. The DVLA barely acknowledges their existence, neither issuing nor offering for sale 'zero' numbers – because, it says, of 'obvious scope for confusion'.

Although the registration plate was not the focus of this 1960 Scammell/Albion factory photograph, the tractor unit carries old-style, Lancashire-issued, 'general' trade plates, with white letters on a darker (red) background. These were superseded by what are now recognised simply as 'trade plates', featuring red lettering on a white background.

27

The 2001 registration system is not carried over to trade plates, which still use area identifiers from the earlier system, with up to three numbers followed by two letters. Trade-plate numbers below 100 feature 'leading zeros'. Here a trade plate issued by the Bedford Vehicle Registration Office is attached to a Vauxhall Vectra carrying an interesting plate of its own.

Q registrations were long used for vehicles temporarily imported into mainland Britain. This Volvo 121 estate car arrived in Britain in October 1963 for press evaluation before the model went on sale. Destined eventually to return to Sweden, it carries a two-letter, four-figure QH registration and is a classic example of why Q registrations were needed.

further Q combinations) were allocated to temporarily imported vehicles following the established two-letter, four-number sequence, later moving to three letters and three numbers. Diminishing numbers of Q plates were also issued with year suffixes and prefixes, and latterly these came to signify vehicles of indeterminate age rather than a temporary import.

In Ireland, the ZZ registration marked a temporarily imported vehicle. Although Q-plated cars were occasionally seen on British roads in the 1960s and 1970s, plates denoting temporary importation (as opposed to vehicles of indeterminate age) have become very rare. Identifiers XA through to XF were originally allocated for issue within London, but during the 1960s the growing shortage of marks led to their reassignment to various other authorities. After 1974, all X-series identifiers were gradually withdrawn, though one or two series were used on vehicles destined ultimately for permanent VAT-free export. In the system introduced in September 2001, X identifiers are designated for the same purpose.

Interesting and special combinations

A number of registration idiosyncrasies have appeared over the years – some dating well back in time; others being relatively recent, Government-inspired 'wild cards'. For a long while, the combination GPO was allocated to Post Office vehicles – until the number of vehicles run by that body exceeded 999! The registration USN became a United States Navy series and was no longer issued in Dunbartonshire, where it had originally been allocated, and similar fates befell combinations involving the letters RAF and USA. For many years, in some parts of the country, ambulances, police cars and fire appliances could regularly be seen with registration marks including the figures 999.

Royal vehicles

Limousines used on official engagements and formal occasions by the sovereign are the

Above left: *In the past, emergency vehicles often bore 999 registration numbers. This immaculately turned-out, privately owned Leyland fire tender was first registered in the Plymouth area, where it operated during its working life.*

Above right: *This vehicle, operated by the Ottery St Mary and District Hospital League of Friends in Devon, continues an old tradition, combining the old emergency-services registration number 999 with specially selected letters OSM, for the hospital's home town. These letters would once have indicated Scottish origins – SM was issued for many years by Dumfries County Council.*

In 2002 just six royal limousines carried no registration number, though in earlier times this unique concession may have been more liberally interpreted. Here, King Edward VII is at the wheel of his 1907 Daimler, without a number plate, trying out a then new dust-reducing road surface called Ermenite.

The royal Bentley presented to Her Majesty the Queen on 29th May 2002 to mark the Golden Jubilee. This vehicle was used extensively during the Queen's Golden Jubilee tour – and, like the five Rolls-Royces in the royal fleet also used on state occasions, the new Bentley does not carry a registration number.

only vehicles in Britain not required to carry registration numbers, because they fall outside the scope of the Vehicle Excise and Registration Acts. Five Rolls-Royces built respectively in 1948, 1960, 1961, 1978 and 1987, together with a Bentley presented to Her Majesty the Queen on 29th May 2002, were at the end of 2002 the only royal vehicles that carried no registration plates. Vehicles used personally by members of the royal family carry registration marks in the normal way.

Military vehicles

Vehicles of the armed forces have long utilised their own special registration system, unrelated to the public system of registration marks. Plates on such vehicles continue in the earlier original style, with paired silver or white characters on a black background – rather than black characters on a yellow or white reflective background, as used elsewhere since 1973.

Auctions

Since 1989, the British Government has capitalised on a steadily growing market in sales of 'desirable' registration numbers. Some (but by no means all) of its vast stock of unused or long-dormant registration numbers is now regularly offered for sale, at auction or over the telephone, on a 'buy the number you want' basis. Prices in 2003 ran from £250, though most fell between £1000 and £5000. One of the first such registration numbers to be sold was '1 A', costing £200,000 – but the all-time record price was reached in 1993, when 'K1 NGS' went at auction for £231,000. Such figures must have made 'COL 1N' seem like a bargain at £76,500 in January 1999, though lower sums have been seen: 'BOB 8Y' realised £19,000, 'TOP 501L' £12,200 and 'DEN 715T' a mere £10,500 during 2002. Yet, with over a million registrations sold and over £500 million raised at the end of 2001, the sale of marks remains a useful revenue generator for the Treasury.

Anomalies

From the earliest days, allocations including the letters I and Z went to Ireland, whilst S was allocated to Scotland, with G and V also briefly carrying unique Scottish status. Early two-letter allocations did not therefore include second-letter G marks, though later there were several such (haphazard) Scottish allocations – AG went to Ayr, FG to Fife, Aberdeen got RG, and Stirling got WG. With S, G, V, I and Z earmarked for specific Scottish and Irish geographic areas, the combinations of GI, IG, II, VI, IV, SI, IS and ZS would have had unacceptably mixed Irish and Scottish overtones and so remained unused. One 'mixed nationality' combination that was used, however, was SZ, allocated to County Down as pressure for further Northern Ireland registration marks gradually increased.

Certain marks have deliberately never seen the light of day, usually for obvious reasons: Leeds never issued any BUM combinations, for instance, and Devon was always mysteriously coy about issuing SOD. Great Yarmouth County Borough Council never mentioned SEX, and Birmingham always seemed very sensitive about DOG. Several seemingly 'normal' combinations were withheld in the early twentieth century, because it was felt that the connotations might offend a sensitive public still steeped in Victorian values. Early marks held back – but later used – included DT, GR and DD. The combinations OO and WC were

avoided for much longer, until the 1960s registration-mark shortage became so acute that Essex County Council was allocated both prefixes. In those days, before James Bond films had hit the silver screen, registrations were issued on a 'just as they come' basis, and so the OO sequence

For many years, registrations involving 'OO' were avoided as a possible source of confusion. Eventually, pressure for more area codes saw OO combinations used – continuing until shortly before the arrival of the new system. This Essex-registered 1989 Ford Sierra estate is a rare 2.9 litre V6 4x4 version.

commenced at OO 1. It therefore follows that a very valuable OO 7 is probably still out there somewhere.

Aside from those combinations involving I, Q, S and Z already mentioned, virtually all possible series of single- and two-letter codes, followed by up to four figures, were eventually issued. That was not the case, however, with many 'reversed' versions of such marks, strings of which have surfaced in DVLA auctions held since 1989.

One number is especially quirky: 666 was used on plates for almost eighty years, but was withdrawn in 1990 following press and public concern about drivers' unexplained misfortunes – and possible connections with the devil. Earlier 666 registrations remain valid, and unissued 666 combinations can be purchased from the DVLA sale of marks section.

The great mistake...

Although care was taken in the early years to avoid issuing offensive combinations, the 1903 issue of marks saw Dorset County Council allocated BF. Though it now seems trivial, this caused a public outcry amongst some of the citizens of that county, and Dorset rapidly and successfully applied for another combination. It was given the FX registration, which came into use early in 1905.

Re-registration was not compulsory when FX was introduced, but around a quarter of Dorset's motorists took up an offer to change their BF registrations. Fifteen years later, however, the Roads Act of 1920 withdrew the few BF numbers remaining in use, obliging owners to re-register in order to gain mandatory FX allocations. Many years later, with sensitivities less acute and combinations becoming scarce, BF resurfaced, with Staffordshire County Council allotted this controversial series – and absolutely no recorded fuss then or since.

The Ormonde motorcycle to which the unfortunate BF 1 was allocated still exists, residing on loan at the Haynes Motor Museum in Somerset. The machine's original registration was both allocated to it and later transferred by its first owner, Edward A. Ffooks, the Dorset County Solicitor, then a resident of Sherborne. The machine gained Y 5 as its replacement registration, which was later sold, leaving the Ormonde with the anonymity of an age-related BS plate. The combination BF 1 was still in use during 2001, and 1 BF was sold in the DVLA's cherished marks auction in September of that year – for £21,400.

1963 was a memorable year for vehicle registrations, as some licensing authorities started issuing their first suffix plates. This Middlesex 'A' plate is attached to a rare Hillman Super Minx estate car.

Further reading

Hill, Tony. *The A to Z of Car Numbers.* Hartley Publications, 1985.

Riden, Philip. *How to Trace the History of Your Car.* Merton Priory Press, 1991 and 1998.

Robson, Peter. *Car Registrations in the British Isles.* Newby Books, 2003.

Rowe, R. G. *What's That New Mark?* Venture Publications, 2001.

Speechley, Ruby. *Fanatical about Number Plates.* Regtransfers.co.uk, 2002.

Woodall, Brian, and Heaton, Brian. *Where's It From? When Was It Issued?* Car Number Galaxy Publications, 1994.

Woodall, Noel, and Heaton, Brian. *Car Numbers.* Car Number Galaxy Publications, 1992, 1995 and 2000.

From 1934 until 2001, Glass's Guide published an annual handbook, *Index of Vehicle Registration Marks.* Copies of each issue have been deposited at the British Library, Boston Spa, Wetherby LS23 7BY. Telephone: 01937 546060.

A regular Newsletter and website covering the world of car registrations is operated by the Registration Numbers Club, PO Box MT12, Leeds LS17 7UD. Telephone: 0113 226 7497. Website: www.registrationnumbersclub.org.uk

A range of helpful leaflets on the background to registering and re-registering old and new vehicles is available from the Driver and Vehicle Licensing Agency, Swansea SA6 7JL. Customer enquiry unit telephone: 0870 240 0010. Further information is available on the DVLA website, at www.dvla.gov.uk and at www.motoring.gov.uk

ACKNOWLEDGEMENTS

The support of the Michael Sedgwick Trust in the publication of this Shire book is very much appreciated. I am also indebted to a long list of people who have contributed information, encouragement, observations and advice, as well as posing some tantalisingly interesting questions (not all of which currently have answers) about the foibles of the British vehicle registration system.

Only some of the many are mentioned here, particularly: Nick Baldwin, Wynne Keenan and the Press Office team at DVLA Swansea, Richard Freeman, Andrew Morland, Bob Wright at the Ford Motor Company, John Lefley at Volvo, Wayne Bruce at Nissan, Michael Ware, and Geoff Smith and Jim Whyman of the Federation of British Historic Vehicle Clubs. Thanks also to Nigel Simms, owner of the Ormonde motorcycle originally registered BF 1, and to the Haynes Motor Museum for allowing it to be photographed.

Most photographs in this book are from the author's collection, excepting those on the cover, provided by the Ford Motor Company, Volvo Car UK and Volkswagen GB Ltd, and on pages 1 and 12, which appear by courtesy of the AA, and page 26, by courtesy of Nissan Motor GB Ltd. The photograph on page 1 is by Dave Portus Photography and that on page 23 (top) by John Dunbar.